SAME FACES

Books by Albert Mobilio

Games and Stunts (2017)
Touch Wood (2011)
Me with Animal Towering (2002)
The Geographics (1995)
Bendable Siege (1991)

SAME FACES

BSE

ISBN: 978-0-9997028-6-4

BSE Books are distributed by
 Small Press Distribution
 1341 Seventh Street
 Berkeley, CA 94710
 orders@spdbooks.org | www.spdbooks.org
 1-800-869-7553

BSE Books can also be purchased at
www.blacksquareeditions.org and www.hyperallergic.com

Contributions to BSE can be made to
 Off the Park Press, Inc.
 976 Kensington Ave.
 Plainfield, NJ 07060
 (Please make checks payable to Off the Park Press, Inc.)

To contact the Press please write:
 Black Square Editions
 1200 Broadway, Suite 3C
 New York, NY 10001

An independent subsidiary of Off the Park Press, Inc.
Member of CLMP.

Publisher: John Yau
Editors: Ronna Lebo and Boni Joi
Design & composition: Shanna Compton

Cover art: *Double Portrait with Frames* (1960) by Alex Katz. Oil on board,
20 x 31½ inches. By permission of the artist.

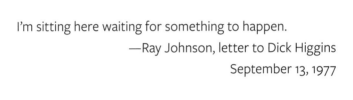

I'm sitting here waiting for something to happen.

—Ray Johnson, letter to Dick Higgins
September 13, 1977

Contents

For Joseph Donahue

I.

Triumph of Poverty

What did I suppose when they beckoned?
A road we'd be surrounded by?
Such strange flora, my pockets inside out.
Come rest your clothes while I rest mine.

What graph demonstrates that we're improving?
There's a newer model in the catalog.
We drive, carry, then drive further.
Sky crowded with gray—metal rubbed in soot.

The decorations are sagging, the dance is over.
Longing on faces, faces hung like freight;
Gaze entertained by an incessant to-and-fro.
According to experts, heredity is our factor.

What's the story they tell about strangers at doors?
Zero times zero performs a scurrying sound;
Among monuments no one can bend.
What's usable gets used, the rest left out to rot.

In the Wild

Don't be afraid that we have begun this
experiment in giving ourselves
the sweetie-size kiss
meant for helpless flesh.

You won't appreciate our appetite
for rumors, for the smudged hours
when swallowing is heard & our
drainpipe error awaits us.

Have you read about the bloody seed?
About the teeth of the literati?
My fingers thick with glue, my head
bound up in greasy sheets.

Banish qualms about your moronic costume—
the teasing way you pitch your woo
won't diminish the grace with which
your savage day awakens.

Come on, we can't wait for whatever you
want us to wait for; we're braced
to beat the clock with muscle-might &
string-bean arms.

Don't be afraid to pity us, with our swollen
peach & curdled need to please—
we're quite the sight among the brooding
stares of slow & slowly ticking beasts.

Amphitheater

Bone-colored hats provided shelter
from the heat; each stone

bench required its own way
of walking toward it.

Small commotions among children
caused a few to call out.

Many came to see string tied &
untied & tied again; others

came because their newspapers
were tired of being read.

They watched scenes animated by
tattered drums & bouquets

gathered by girls along the path.
They came & carried themselves

as soldiers do & they studied
how to say *farewell* &

to listen to that word as it falls
from highest to lowest steps.

The sky was worn as if it were a coat;
the flutes from the stage

conjured aloneness; their melodies hard
to remember. They came

for that & they sat with each other
& said these are trees,

& those are the trees, too.
When morning sunlight flickered

on wet grass they filed out, each bearing
a portion of the hero's dying vow

into streets & venerable parlors, shards
of singing left behind.

Halfway

halfway restless, hung upon
the mist soon

pushed into
devouring sun, it's impossible

to restore what isn't
yet lost, isn't attainable

either. there's no point
in lifting the self-

made dross, the daft
creed you use to jump start

your slack fervor; leave
the house, bow

further the head that's slipping
steep. you can't write

about that, you can't begin to
imitate if your thoughts

hover mute above painted seas.
now there's a metaphor that might

caress this meager strife, devise
a viable gimmick: more

impulse, more accidental
syntax in the breakers—

small seas brimming over
into larger, somehow slanted ones.

thus equipped, you might set sail
in such obscuring weather.

Initiation Rite

Look at what we're doing to the mileage.
We get that way by giving into crave.

Imagine us cooking in the woods—the ladle,
the fire, the jagged lid of an open can.

Twilight unsettles us, sparks fly up toward
the firmament; they only strengthen

the darkness by revealing what little
there is that isn't void.

Between my thumb & forefinger, between
this & what's permissible: the mortal

twitch of things—surviving what first
alights as choice then later as cost.

Laurels for wide-awake clarity
in such a face-stained trance—the flag

ceremony is about to start. Birds move
in ever-tightening circles too fast

to describe, while the banner whips madly
in otherwise fallow air.

I handle figures in carpets, holy wrath;
but reliving the past

isn't what it used to be; the souvenirs—
novels, deliriums, slide rules—are broke

from overuse. Breeze blows this way or that,
the duration of earthly pulse.

Is a surprise still surprising if I brought
the party hats? Watch me get almost free

of this hoodoo system, ready to live
where never happens to be now.

Moods at Noon

I was rude to the king of soap.
My childhood is no excuse or even
the source of blame.

One loses sight of enthusiasms.
My precautions kept guard over me,
while I let others smoke stylishly.

In consequence, my thoughts were trivial,
commonplace. I was a neutral person so
I decided to undergo an operation.

Voices drifted in from the waiting room
& pumps pumped something new
where it supposedly would do its best.

People, I'm told, who went to very good
colleges had their hands in it,
but still, again, I was rude to the king of soap.

Every day a bit older; useless to brood
more than you have to or try
untangling motive from its synapse.

I found small bewilderments like candy
in my lunch bag. They were sticky & they
spoiled my precious subjectivity.

There's nothing worth saying to this king,
his ministers, his mopey
wife of soap.

The smear of lipstick, the grimy crown.
To serve the pleasure of this dawdler king,
I genuflect then slightly clown.

Informal Lull

Days I was a live wire there was nothing
I wouldn't push up against: the washboard, binary law
& several post-its pasted

in the new world's teenage diary.

I slew me myriads & pranced pompous-like.
My arrow—sketched to symbolize vengeance—
startled a stranger, his mitts already

busy in the poor box that's mine to steal from.
Almost everyone—their oaths flung to dirt,
& their charred gowns flaunted
in all the pity places—was an insult to be borne,

even as that realization was only newly mine.

Then crept upon me: immediacies,
& their snug fit inside my pipe-shaped woe.
I lacked an air of authority or an authority

over the air, either way

my nervous system's geography was cribbed
from a pamphlet about the afterlife of dogs.
Then the breakup: knees first,

crushing all literary intentions, the ones I made up

during the outdoor exercise period.
Consider this biscuit-gnawing guest, my streak
of mud mussed her skirt; our embrace

within a labyrinth of dusks. We are but a sliver

of willowy height is what I whispered & there
began her refusal clock with its heavy
tock & pointy tick.

Her tearful peepers lit shiny by my miner's lamp.
The congregation wearing wigs, their wizened
miens all tanned, kept warm amid icy

virtues. A good deal for us—regrets traded

for milk of human kindness; doesn't matter
if it's spilled, she'll wring the mop dry
& then lofty, cleanly we will be.

Where went that egghead look you do?

We'll park for free in the all-day lot then dine
on the dusty praise we're used to,
yet wouldn't you guess—

above us those damn clouds dragging

themselves through another ineloquent sky.
Her refrain: our moment leashed to tides,
what going out leaves behind.

Worry shrewdly brings me round: we'll shoulder

this problem as if wind held us in our shoes.
This display of us, bone sturdy we won't
fall, yet we stand too heart-bent

to much alleviate the chore.

Notebook Entry

There was talk about the size
of what we would admit it was
& that was alright with me. I didn't care

if we used the long kind
of description or the shorter, snappier
taste of the thing. Either way,

it seemed to me, you got the gist,
the overall commotion. A moon, however
dappled with elegant phrases,

is no more than a moon. And the ruminative
consequence—the sense of having seen
what was said—isn't any

deeper than if you press yourself smack
against the spectacle, gaze up
through high-tension lines & grasp

its patient force because it's big, isn't it?
And no explanation, adumbration,
no mere disaster of pages tells

of summer expanse, prop plane chewing
at the emptiness, fists of faraway smoke
opening & then gone. I was making

my mark, was taking time off to estimate
from here to where it's better
to sit when the chair came into view,

wooden, painted white, the one you think
about & there it is—
allocated from a familiar stage, once

occupied by the baffled doctor or hard-ass cop
who played their parts as if
that chair weren't as much mine as theirs &

the mark I made wasn't as clear as their faces
in moonlight. The size of chairs, of moons &
motorbikes & salt shakers

won't fit on a list of things to buy next time
I drive to town & stand slack-jawed
at the counter, confiding

less than planned & more than
I should, bold phrases gaining altitude
around my scribbling head.

Forest for Trees

What use are you, not even
knowing the names

of flowers or able
to discern whether breaking

branches or backfire wracks
your nights? The pastoral's more

intricate than couplets teach:
there are stoic forms that keep

proper distance between mountain
& mountainous.

These fields burn, their flames
a lustrous verdict

that this meadow sways toward.
What use are you, never

caring to apprehend this path,
its scuffs, strewn stalks

& flesh smooth leaves, the whirring
ground they cloak?

The Passersby Pass By

A dowsing fiasco causes a mob to gather
around the perforation. They disarm the fiddler;

& divide up the quiet parts of his instrument.
Eventuality was what they labeled it later on.

Let's cozy up to the jukebox, swing changeable
amidst, forestall this house from ending

up mouthy squawking wall-to-wall.
Unruly cakewalk then first-aid kits; the hurly,

the burly, the cops in several sizes, the burden
we're endeared to. Middling fun at best

but the trailing disappointments glint like orbits
of a planetarium's spheres.

This clock is really a camera filming photos
of credible wilderness for the aesthetes back home.

Vibration's my camouflage; I'm nestled swell
in a theme park log flume. Pinholes help

with seeing, but you have to poke your own.
Gentle votary manipulate the scene; count

the saturns & plutos, our sprawled bequest
of voyage. Everyone who's anyone

now finds the lawn, the lawn chairs, too.
Chimes ring tall as nervy, lustful gloom ensues.

Faults in Place

Before the curtain rose he confirmed life
requires distraction; you don't

want to be cold, to be blithe,
he said seeming aware

that his nervous satisfactions were plainly
in evidence. His charm depended

on making palaver from the unattended
needs of those around him.

The chief source of strong feelings,
a machine for condensing

& storing up pleasure, sorrows. He heard
them announce his steam room

future: another ex-virtuoso sobbing about
how obvious everyone else is.

An outcome of his misdeeds? They amount
to what? An envelope stuffed

with fits & starts unfit for modern
reading? The curtain was raised & he

portrayed a man common as dirt whose soul
blew in from the kitchen, whose ever-

fleeting slap wasn't kind or talked
about; the scenes he played—

vigorously mourning the loss
of a porkpie hat—failed to tighten

around even one memory. Instead, he bent
sensation, made us feel ourselves

as shadows breeding shadows, that profligacy
growing wilder on the sly.

Saying as You Do

don't be what you aren't, saying as you do,
saying sorry because

& there's always a *because* isn't there,
good reasons why, same reasons, mostly.

admission's meant to be a saving fact,
but saving what? honest should

be more than lack of caution, but christ,
not really if it torpedoes

what we could possibly think
through, figure out how much a shackle

forgiving is or find less busted
tricks; but we both do love our move:

hard arrival & departure at this ongoing
place of propped up tears

An Implication

Look what happened to my broken toaster. No one fathoms the distress I endured when it died.

I don't have the connective tissue that enables me to wear my own face without distraction; hence, I am a ringer for myself.

When I read in a novel the expression *actual sex* I thought *swarm of bees*. The toaster is broken & maybe that explains it.

We know enough about our own hands to use them but not enough to leave them alone.

The mail is too large for my mailbox so I've stopped waiting. Guys in black jackets—that show's always in reruns.

My somber kernel of doubt is unlikeable. The toast used to rhyme like olden-made poems & now it's prose.

Class Dismissed

How goes your midnight boost-up, mister gloom?
You don't like me asking, do you?

Study hour is over & it's time to test your skills.
Your luminous climes are exhausted having
been excessively lived through.
Prepare for the elation that comes from
repeating "Life is oh so awkward."

The hour for agitated repose begins the way
the others did only this one brings
its own bad news. You can bathe, can't you

mister my-o-my, in the coolness
your cupped hands make for your face?
It's time to lose that sneer & start
again with nada but those riddles
inside soda bottle caps. The hour to be at fault

has come around: the stars pose as mementos
of spiritual renewal. Description is often all
you have to work with, the modifier

modifying some famously important noun.
Ho-hum. No one's looking, mister murky-stew,
so make what you can from that.

Salutation

Bare torso stone-like in the sand, empty
bottles glint beside. What can spring

us from this unceasing beach faster
than the measuring game?

Wordy scuffle in the fretful lair; our zeal
boxed for easy handling &

our tunes turned toward the night's selector.
Sufficient speakage for that tiny phone,

but you get good heaps of fight that way.
Beauty learns which gears do

sentimental work: that boring page
of rules. Our stunts include plummeting

from curbstones & tearing out random pages
from the bookshelves of friends.

Carry mirrors into the high, brown grass
to show the season what it can do

when it isn't even trying. Unmarked feelings
weigh the same as those with name tags.

The headstones aren't serious in the way
manuals of know-how can be.

Chips off the thrashing anima get caught
up in our combs. We're humble

at the starting line, heel-draggers, but
that's our racket. Cue the water-

works, kiddo.

Cross Cut

Better dry than take refuge within the brawn
of those who disobey the clouds

because they are innumerable & I am not.
The boatman has an illustrated tale

of his own and his earnestness is evident.
Inquiries should be made about the outdoor

version of our innermost parts—but no one
will be pleased if you stand

up at the high-school assembly & say,
weren't those dead brothers just unlucky.

But that was the pack that I ran with when I ran
that way, brandished a knotty stick

& rolled newspapers for the flue.
I lacked big-picture cognizance even

as my saga took shape from pocket trash
& genteel sips of discontent.

Missive

The envelope in which the comet arrived. The veil
between this world and what comes next.

The spare key in that man's shoe. His knowledge
had roamed as far as it could before failing.

A grave among obelisks. What might sharpen these
self-evident splendors?

The knife that opened the sky broke against stone.
He came singing at first, then not.

A word repeated then diminished by air carrying
the smell of cut grass.

Behind the shed, the shed behind the heap:
the tender thing, his summoning light.

Categories of Apprehension

The tension rubbed the skin wrong ways & so
resort to that muddy snooze

you laid all day inside of.
Take out that serenity stone by the glimpse

of thee, the bound up place
where we are housed & insist *solve this, dipshit*

●

They go to trial because they normally do, shades
of emotional crimes pinned on me; or maybe

you are unsatisfied with your enemies. They were
workable types you could learn from

their tangled, downward folds, vacant inside
except the cookie's good crumb

●

Can you steer? Could they be a plentitude
of spectacular winds? You raise

your eyes: what's this laughing around
sleek-faced boys pissing in a stream. Holler now

at passing trains, feel weak as possible without
falling through the mouth you live with

●

They had another year of electricity to use
like you use rocks, picked up & flung far

but still visible & they inhabit the scrapes
the air endures. Switch worlds or be overly averse to

fight good fights, you listen when told to button up,
to broom this wilderness

●

We're on the lookout for a surefire cure—phony
grandeur is contagious, seeps into our gathered,

utmost selves. Nobody wants a static, bookish thing
that doesn't get devotional; are you

wise to this or do you find the feeling of aboveness
difficult to describe at your schooled remove

●

The giveaway clue held tight
to the breast you have been among

orphic squads their noises rush by, shedding
xeroxes. The trivial light they wear

seldom collects into larger vindications, instead
remaining vague & ever aimless

●

The freshly scattered handbills caught in fences,
pressed against windshields: the yard sale

drama isn't humdrum anymore. We grow tired
on the lower rungs latticed

by neurologic calm—but who redeems themselves
that they should be who no one ever was

●

This moon reclines in autumn's reverie our battered
limbs hang robespierre in flirty scenes.

Posing at the subway station, sheer absorption,
despite this pleading, that praising, we're voice-

less & headed in the wrong direction—you've surely
seen us collide this way before

Signal Scene

Unfurl for us what to believe: fears, wishes,
opinions, we will never
rise above them. The very language
is not readily enlarged

by action; replay in high definition
delivers that sort of transcendence.
Surviving the gorgeous nonstop crash
requires an agile tenderness.

Burn brightly, you minor bits of fun.
Earth heaped up & from there
we can observe what happens
down among those stately

yet ordinary fellows. We unbend
what they complete—their scenes flow
fluently when the decorative vases &
bushes are given speaking parts.

Do we understand anything at all about
these views of life? Their nonchalance so
out of place, that muzak sensation
slick on every revelation.

I talked about trembling weeds &
asked the radio where I was born.
We were teased about being scared,
about the harm our possessions do.

There must be someone we aren't anxious
to be alone with or perhaps a kind
of question that isn't built
for answers overheard in elevators.

Kingdom Come

You could say we were joined at the hip &
that we'd never roam the plains
like people who roam plains now or used to.

Speaking of that bygone time brought nettle-
sharp silence to the brutes who survey us
from their ancestral heights.

Should we yearn to be thrown a loving bone?
It's dandy to ask *who done it*
when the carnage crew comes knocking.

We were penitents unmoored by a new kind
of meditation that mixed up *trust*,
hushed, and *must* & you wouldn't believe how

funny that looked in the family album.
I wanted us to hide in a crawl space
where our lives would be open books no

one could read in the dark—a dissolving
realm where the utterance trough
has been scoured clean.

Our plan: to dig among the relics
for the one we can forsake. What furtive gleam
then in these my errant hands.

Wanderers

These sad beliefs are knickknacks
in need of dust so we can honor their longevity

This sanity whets our common blade, its purities
beheld when something's cut

You situate yourself among tenuous proclamations
no more plausible for the suddenness with
which they are made

These metal-tasting pills you turn away from—
but hold them, keep them & everyone, you suspect,
sleeps in the same kind of dark

This hand traced in water isn't faltering, isn't guilty
yet there remains its elusive force

We kept dry on the porch as the storm boomed out
of reach, our thinking gone to untallied sums

You didn't care about whether risk could be
taken in & then exhaled: smear of cirrus on night's
impatient, restless luster

Dreary occasions spent posing: however strong
we set our chins the photos lacked plot &
we failed to be familiar to ourselves

The treatments you get may not explain the problem
but they restore your grasp of its lexicon

II.
The Same Faces You Can't Believe In

"Film after film, subject after subject, confronting
the same faces that one cannot believe in."
—Robert Bresson, *Notes on the Cinematographer*

This dancer is out

This dancer is out of step with that one whenever
the mood makes you wish you
weren't as devout as you are your mental
equipment dependent on bread crumbs, wire
& pigeons come home to roost in hairline
cracks only visible when very near to sense
the empty knell our puny human strike allows

The nightfall was beauty was strange in its hills,
its desolations penciled on scrap paper,
letters to ancestors & you have become over
aware of revolutionary movements their history
bursting with cell block scenes & mispronunciations
of dirty words the greedy camera's
focus pulling back though the actor isn't pleased

You bet on this skirmish among heavens they
attract indifferently but that's the loneliness
of sand that's nothing to me & thoughts
by the millions go begging, truly an exalted life
you're giving yourself to the agitated air,
smug boots & mock sensation: who are your gods,
are they the ones that fight the daytime's fire

this dancer

step whenever
the mood makes

your mental
       crumbs
              come home
visible to sense
the empty human

nightfall was
scrap paper,
you have
         history
bursting with mispronunciations

dirty, greedy,
pleased:
heaven—
that's the loneliness

of nothing & thoughts
      exalted

the agitated,
smug gods
       are fire

A resemblance between rivers

A resemblance between rivers their curves they endure
soft handed clutch from bank to bank he's well
lit alone a sailor steeped in surf he woke up his psyche
prepared his dipstick to plumb jars
of murky tokes & this browsing from
a great height he remembers methods for sorting
recognitions, those ferried over from leafy shores

His elocution was brought to bear upon
his everyday systems the sublunary world
he signed up for & showed he was partial to,
a fan of classical art, columns, plinths,
those serene marble contours that's what the kids
go for, they tied him in a magical knot
in the scholastic manner those silly joys strike awe

Don't bounce don't drop these heavy matters more
than they can stand their flaws might yield
results you can't imagine he needs to save
those thoughts, the ones like hallways with doors
shut to hometown nomads & the sound of distant
footsteps coming nearer maybe heading
into the brain-sized geometry he's adorned within

between rivers

curves they endure
                        soft
lit in his psyche
prepared to
row,
he remembers
cognition

upon
the world
he signed
columns, plinths,
those serene contours
tied him in

joy

matters more
than flaws
he needs to save
                        one
                & sound distant
                        steps:

the geometry's within

By the time summer arrived

By the time summer arrived he knew he was a long
digression in everyone else's argument even
though he drank a beer quickly to chase
off the smell of burned up worlds he should have
set the toaster on medium but outtalked is why
he found himself stuck in what old doc grady
dubbed *a painful marital situation*

Has anything changed he occupies an upstairs
attitude this man of intelligence who requires above
all that his quiet remain free of tarnish & smashing
that blockhead is at most another fading
soul complaining that submission hurts when
you get turned down, face flushed your american-
made cock sent back to the guidance office

His tokens of love kept hidden their tongue-tied
majesty locked away they stink up the joint
with dolorous musk he's too close
to lie about better to slide inside that memory
palace a shack of metal rain like spit out
teeth pelt the roof the bile it's impossible not to savor
that angels fight for nickels overhead

the time

summer was
everyone else's
to chase

the burned worlds he
                talked is why
he found himself
painful

upstairs
this man
free of tarnish, ash

another fading
mission:
you get turned your
            mad dance
is hidden
locked up
            too close
to lie inside memory

spit out
bile, impossible
                angel

Maybe it started

Maybe it started as a joke the apparitions, the decorative
locusts no beast could resist you had to laugh
didn't you conclude this was a good sign brought
forth out of otherwise impenetrable noise, two bent
horns that's spike jones at the bandstand please
raise your lamp to comprehend every creeping
thing that seems, yet seems not so flung as wind

I had a notion what my god would look like all done
up in sunday best really smart with skinny
tie & cufflinks shiny even in home movies
where you play kamikaze & only ten were left
out of thousands who began with worshipful minds
but ended up beneath the stage their grim science
just some reed they hope will tuneful lie

A nod in the right direction, the sullied bed the eerie
premonition my device warns me cover
those tracks never explain the squint cloaked
in discouragement how stand such solitude,
no haunting face to put my heart to work I scratch,
kick & bite then picture an altar that reveals
the vacant depth to which I fall when falling

maybe

a joke
you had to laugh,
conclude this was
    impenetrable, bent

              please
comprehend every
thing as wind

my god:
smart,
shiny even
    you play
with worshipful minds,
but the stage grim:
    some hope
        in sullied bed

my vice—
    ever plain—
rage, solitude
no heart:

picture an altar
    falling

Torches line the road

Torches line the road to barren ground we will
be sentimental there about daffy, yosemite
sam & tweety bird the onlookers will be patients
who've given samples & given up we won't
lip-sync what matters to us should be what matters
to the gang safe on the balcony casting their bold
gander on our procession, their cheers wet with petals

You learned me good that my physiology was yours
to counterfeit for profit to use as you please
save me from battling the mad scientist the survivor
rules the termite rodeo my midnight show's bit
players chew scenery, extinguish illusions about how
easily what's human succumbs to metamorphosis,
the corruption that assails each dream's waking

Movie names should be recited when you can't
nod off you can say them to yourself instead
of squirming in the dark your head between pillows
& your thoughts like crows chased from ledges
flying off every which way I pretend not to notice
the pharmacy in your drawer, the insatiable maw
drinks deep whatever bleeds stranger than we do

the road

barren ground: we will
be sent there,
      onlookers
who've given
       what matters—
safe casting
     our petals

you learned
to count to
save me: the survivor
      rules
         illusion
(what human
waking)

names—
say them instead
of squirming between
thoughts
      flying to

your raw insatiable
     anger

How prove each soul

How prove each soul she called last night with news
that a problem might arise
among members of the insect class, for instance,
moths who dined on her marine-blue jacket,
then silverfish darting across the bathtub's white
tundra, each trusty emissary brings
attention to itself, she noted, ensuring its demise

We commemorate the lounge all booze & sticky
voices spilled emotion staining fivers
on the bar she bought another round, inconstant
goes our creator's mission nothing
less than change immense we always stare
headlong into the barroom's oscillating fan its ever-
humming negative our point of last departure

Her shadow explains the sum of its extinctions, long
forgotten but those junkyard scars they mark
you, get you sick with a pinch of powder, pinch
of pathos to shine the grass-combed wind that's split
by steeples she remembers how
wings skittered as she flew far across herself
her airborne bones were thin as dusk

how each

soul

might arise

among instances

blue
then silver
tundra

itself its demise

booze & sticky
emotion—

another con

miss nothing
less than immense, stare

into its ever-

humming point

shadow sum of
scars they mark

you, get you

to shine—the wind
remembers how
wings flew far,

born as dusk

I make electricity work

I make electricity work for you or you can strike
matches & curse the darkness there's physical
effort involved in leaving well enough alone outside
the hymn of the pale sea its particles of pristine mist
swarm with your own inhalations the warmth
spent quickly & you hesitate, don't you know
indefiniteness is required for exaltation

Puzzle pieces scattered on the floor don't try solving
when only lunatics keep track of what was said or who
did that dismal turn in the boy's locker room waving
as if he was sailing off bound for remotest
zanzibar close up shot of ship's horn added long after
the extras cashed their checks they waved big *bon
voyages* quite bored & shuffling on the soundstage floor

The story's *marked by a naturalness* that's okay to get
us started but a childish method shouldn't be set
against hostile tactics so you'd better not be adrift
in a half-remembered dawn, eyes veiled
in vaporous trance that won't be the waking up you're
looking for the blood beat switched on & alert
you hear the voice then tense with expectation

make electric

strike
the dark
     alone

the particles of
your own warmth
     hesitate,
          finite

     pieces
of what was said
that turn in the boy

     he was remote
long after
they waved—
          sounds
marked by naturalness

a child shouldn't be,
     better not be, adrift
eyes veiled,
     waking
the beat switched:
you hear the expectation

Promised land on a postcard

Promised land on a postcard its droll parades
found by that busybody who prowls avenues
of sepia-tinted towns, their drowsy
gusts of bronze guitar he's lulled beneath
those bursts of grief, to lose balance
while standing waist-deep in stones yet still
round the block another forlorn day he swept aside

Vines curl, pine trees shudder & thinking seems
a tightrope strung from green-gowned chimney to
higher than this simple man's king more dead than we
the living who used his wood for fuel his shoes for speeding
down that crazy bend those kinds of roads
aren't legal now while regulation makes us sway
on surfaces as steep & hard as noon

Written wings, their smoke-traced architecture made
from pencils held like leaves, like knives, ground
into pliant bits of silver akin to light have you seen
what the sun can do to make this ardor more than
hidden, less than earth its paradox behind your back &
there dwells this nervous, spiny script so changeable
it blows about in quiet, star-hung regions

promised

parades
prowl avenues
drowsy

lulled beneath
balance—
standing stone still
forlorn, he wept
       & thinking seems
strung
higher than
speed

bend,
       now sway—
hard as
written wings
held ground

have you seen
this ardor
hidden behind your
script so
    quiet?

Your heart dulled by passage

Your heart dulled by passage among cruel sprees
the sentences you prepared to sing
draped on jagged branches slippery with dew this
roughness you can't touch a place between one
thing & the sum of things, those named by authors who
believe that naming makes it theirs the raw materials
too heavy to lift into circuitous flow

When you fall you might be seen as sinful your unhurried
motion in full-color magazine spread although
the texture of descent remains unclear these enormous
symptoms ruin the live-let-live paradigm you fought
bravely amid forests with feats of levitation how prideful
going up goes down you were honestly made out
out of liar's stuff a merry hermit diving under stone

Let fear of death retire from your breast, a chamber
of incense, animal skins, is that a lyre & suddenly
we're drowned as stimulated atoms clash
& stammer, flop sweat staining
whoever engulfs us, you kneel before
carnal force its ringing phone you answer
now kill the ache that tastes & smells like gain

hear

passage among
sentences you pare

branches, this
roughness you can't
name

believe the raw
circuitous flow—
fall unhurried,
full
descent unclear:

you fought
levitation
you were made out
of stone,
fear,

suddenly
we're simulated,
sweat
engulfs you—

ringing
the ache, that gain

The judgment scene

The judgment scene was laugh-track time we sought
tension between pulsing, neon bodies, their betrayals
florid, frightening was the sense that human
touch was nothing more than loud more loudly
nights when trouble means an open mouth
divvied out to words so different from their object
you can't circulate one tonality among them

Bleak patch of soil men pulled their faces toward
then turned their faces back the way
they came we get the point—the window, the alley,
the crisscross motion—no one wants to travel
unless the shoulder dips, the hand repeats
whatever hitchhike works & straight again you
see that yonder wall the higher up it goes we're true

In the future our souls as thin as tv shows we wreck
the radiance with disembodied, snake-shaped blaring,
they fill the auditorium & feeble love
there's nothing we can add to except we can
make lists of what deserves to die & various numbered
fates bare-headed days allow
this span of glossy instants profoundly clocked

the scene

we sought
bodies, their betrayal—
that human
was more than *more*

an open mouth,
so different from
tonality among
bleak faces

the way:
the window
no one wants

the hand
works & you
see it goes true

souls wreck
embodied
love

there's nothing except we
die & various numb
fates are
this instant found

Bed narrow & short

Bed narrow & short you can't stretch yourself are you
too nightly bound by brevity sure it's likely
your big-game hunt is past its pretty cartoon brawls
twixt infernal cats & panting mice there's danger
developing on your outer flank since dogmas
often crumble you see all sides
of innocent yet unclothed questions asking still

The campaign thwarted so time to telegraph reluctance
barely felt instead let's nourish doom,
the seducible wife the swankly coiffed husband out
on the patio unpretending saints
they pray to inconceivable dilemmas: swoons &
sullen ecstasies these inward pleasures their humble
gesticulations the fruit the corpus bears

You squander a life same house same ping-pong
game in all the rooms & that tableau
of wild geese in formation above a marsh hanging
like the jesus nightlight kept you safe
but whose kisses & hugs are rightly yours do you
explicate this ignorance can you be found on
the brink of getting off at the far address

be narrow &

are you
too bound;
your game pretty?
there's danger
since
you see
innocent questions still

time to telegraph,
nourish
the seducible
saints

they pray:
        inward their
                gesticulations

you squander life
in rooms
        wild—
the night kept
kisses: yours

can you be found on
the brink of far?

The ideas are ruining

The ideas are ruining the houses she used to visit
against the wishes that once written down are a kind
of turbulence, a disjointed joke fashioned to cause
no harm can occur when she's giving
my flaws a run for their money you couldn't
describe how specters roam her floors, how bones
will be taught in the world to come

Mirror at that angle she can see her face the side she
doesn't know as well she holds her breath & looks
between reflected sighs puts pressure
on her ability to call those deeds they're hardly
going to outlast angels tough enough to suffer
nirvana even its ink is blissful white & sorrow's
fled when opening what used to be untold

Wheels spin in black slush that's how burial goes
far enough for the crowd to perceive whether
the song ended or she just stopped singing then
stood as if curious about nerves, their torn scrap
of surety is really a blindfold slipped over startled eyes
you can't believe conclusions work this system's
loamy hurt in which she grew such self

the ruin

ideas are used—
wishes once written are
turbulence

she's giving
my flaws, you could
roam her
        will in the world

        mirror
her breath & looks
        between pressures

to call
angels to suffer
                sorrow's
untold
        burial

to perceive
        the singing
as nerves, torn
        over—
believe this
hurt

You're not strong enough to save

You're not strong enough to save hours from being
gnawed by their minutes, save sensation
from its dubious weather report that tells little & you
realize there is only the power to choose how to
swerve, not to choose what climate
presses your brow its unkind weight you wear
a cowboy's smirk to fit your daily gun

The prime mover is always going to be around painted
by numbers but people will see existence
the oracular smudge of bruised yellow & didn't
you flinch when you saw your reflection in those frozen-
over contemplations, no spotlight
thrown, nobody influenced your climb he led you
through the fable, phonemes the shape of rocks

An old man somewhere is banging a door a fistful's
worth of life left in him like wispy nylons
hung from the showerhead she left them
as a kind of taunt & you find what might be called
an animal capacity but it's the size of a shirt
pocket too small to kick instinct into gear
you're stuck in shit your hunger about to steer

strong save

you're enough being
        awed by sensation—
                its weather

there is the power to
swerve, to choose
        what weight
            to fit
the always going

people will see
the bruise &
flinch
        over contemplations

nobody led you
through the fable:
        an old man, somewhere,
life left him,
        she left—

you find
        an animal
                instinct
you're stuck in

The thing itself all heaving

The thing itself all heaving flesh I sat wounded
in an unfound sun & was given a flashlight
for the bottomless pit you can't talk me out of
my fascination with how precise
our stumbling is a kind of power I wear this
breastplate made of sapphire & sulfur braced
then for my fragile raid to be overwhelmed

If it's good it's good don't ruin the contrivance with
whole swells of the corporeal you only screw
the spirit out of an airy overture, violins
washing over great men's statues their foreheads
engraved with the motto *Cheap Pearls No*
Money Down you study this as if it were a symptom
I learned your poem but you won't learn mine

A man with a torn scroll & upraised bearing
saturated with his visualization of an actual page
turning to him & according to the clubhouse rules
I pronounced *round* aloud as if I knew
the shape it made in your ear its outer circle full-
fledged yet humble as to-do lists & cheat sheets
get ripped to pieces, that paper that word its ode

in itself

all flesh
was given
    for less—

how precise
I wear this
brace,
    my fragile
        contrivance
of the corporeal

the spirit
washing over statues
engraved with
a symptom:
your poem—
torn & upraised,
    an actual page
      turning

aloud I knew
it in your ear, its full

yet humble
    paper word

In the midst of this widely unread

In the midst of this widely unread life in the line
outside a washroom where truly we are as hollow
as our own confessions those shaken
out of us by close reading tomes about the middle
ages the sun darkening for a dying pope & wintry
scepter jeweled with groans we wore our sexual
sorrow to warm the indentation left in bed

If you wait they play the good songs they have
momentum that clarifies itself amid shouting as
the ambulance arrives we called
ourselves ethereal rising through bluish haze,
the ignorant mouths their nouns around
us—winch, tube, carpet, hive, hiatus—altogether
unreasonably dense these sirens find their mark

The point of philosophy was to save whatever
face we could in this rank incurable
land its spat out river, defiled birds & fingernails
fertile with perplexities we strummed
from our hidden parts the breath glistens
like fresh meat cut, splayed & left for flies we brought
our storm to perfection so it might finally end

the midst of this

unread line
as hollow
as our
reading about
    the dark, dying
    groans we
        left

songs
amid shouting as
we call
    our rising through
the nouns around
us—altogether
dense their
philosophy

    rank
defiled fingers,
we strummed
the breath
brought
to perfection finally

We boozing tired dogs lounge

We boozing tired dogs lounge at our feet with double-
barrel eloquence cocked & ready watch our rebel
tribe smear those gaudy sleeves your pale hand
dusted by sunlight releases the trigger we like how
it all began her disproportionately noisy hair &
foolish worry over what *deep* means when she finds
herself measuring that faceful of lost sleep

Those people were switched around with solitary
folk they play for keeps they fantasize cutting
their rivals to shreds to provide newspapers
with due compensation for the masses already
massing at the gates behind them the broken tower
where a princess discovers her cloistered fate
scrawled in a well-thumbed copy of *The Egoist*

Squeeze hard to sense the urgency my squeaky
ungreased wheel tells how miserable my end must
be or not you can't predict if an astonishing gizmo
might appear its shimmer more eye than sun more
ash than eye & pause the round & round, the filling
up then spending my tired old spy-eyed self
whose turning isn't wrong or even without love

we boozing

tired
        eloquence: watch
your pale
dusted light—release
all air
        deep she finds
                herself, full lost

those people were solitary
                they keep
their shreds,
the masses already
        broken:
                a fate
scrawled in ego

hard to sense my
wheel: how
        astonishing
        its sun
        round & round—
ending tired,
           turning wrong

What good is smoking in the smoking

What good is smoking in the smoking room when talking
isn't allowed where even whispers the ones made
behind cupped hands get shushed but that's not quite
secret what you're telling her: she's familiar to me & don't
brush away all bright creation, my furtive
rings blown round your head they're halos you can
wear them tipped to hide your skeptic seraph

Dial in to skim the textual struggle thick bibles loom
vivid & laugh-a-minute real there's flawless
filth inside us we don't have to greasy lie or show
wallet photos of dumbass teens & dreamy wives
to disclose our thorny crowns in churches we haven't
yet depicted but want words that splatter dark
for this was rosy height undone by what's called toil

The train you missed rolls by its passengers quite
pleased they're punctual they're gaining speed crazy fast
as lives go but slowly this one all baggage-bound
waits yet also serves but serves what & simply
asking this puts you at odds with the engine & its clanging
bell it's too clichéd but that doesn't mean that sound
still doesn't seek out every hollow every ghost

hat king

what is talk—
      whispers
            cupped,
                  familiar
brush away bright
          halos you
               wear to hide
               struggle

& laugh: the flawless
show
of dream,
disclose our own
         words, that ark
               undone

you missed
speed
but slow
        also serves, serves
you with its
bell, that sound
        still ghost

III.
Guide for the Discouraged

Guide for the Discouraged

I'm always taking the test—the cake
I have or the cake people recall
being the best back before
we were overtaken by remorseless now.

The sun can't be stashed in a drawer
just so you can snooze through
its clamor. Look around
at what's called pure
abstraction & try not to think.

I wore slippers in traffic. Then fretted
about the demand to strive; instead,
I realigned with the macrocosm.

An accordion heaves in the garden; how
awful is this allowable shirt.

Sprawling life opened before me
yet it wasn't worth giving
up my steady turn at the faucet.

Come in the spirit of meekness;
leave anointed with blame.

Stupid squirrels. They aren't even
funny as that guy with that hat in line
for pizza. You live bareheaded
until you reckon with your insolence.

Once aloft, the disciples forgotten.
Be careful not to drink
the hope-colored clouds.

There's no mystery. Astronomy
makes us lazy by fixing our sight
on the exit light. Disposable as the sofa
in a dead man's rec room, still
we fruitless scheme.

You made lists of your deceptions & set
them ablaze. Religion has mired you
in the blunder of mere intellect.

Smothered divinity: that's quite a lot
of eschatological ideation
you're putting out with the cat
to wail beneath the crescent
moon tonight.

Draw nigh, the thing unsays itself.

We were walking around the pond when
lumpish love we fell in.
Inclined below & then above.

Why are you doing that, was what I was
asking her when she did what she
wanted to do anyway. Self-abuse, she said,
is turning you against the common good.

Declaim aloud the exploits of one
Theseus the mouse. His *h* was as soft
as his tiny paws in the maze
of mechanical skin.

Was old but not tall enough. They wouldn't
let me ride the ride
so I wept in their pitiless gaze, no Rome
in which I might hide.

Why bother, you cut-rate devil, perjurous
as you are, to pretend? Your Barcalounger
cannot beckon my smithy-made head.

You lost those scars in a cab coming
home from a rooftop party
where you drank to impress—who?

The nurse arrives with an attitude.
She'd rather be administering this shot to
a patient who isn't reciting
the alphabet backwards.

Finality presses upon us daily; we flinch,
then wounded go.

Why am I snared in this routine & why
should I stop if it harms no one & what's
the problem requiring my solution?
Why do birds suddenly appear?

The syndrome: trousers improperly
creased. And wrinkled cuffs.
This hurts, yet realize:
this is how consciousness portrays itself.

Small but noticeable tremors fail
to disturb the bargain hunters. At least
until the tomb cracks wide.

Natural causes—the poise with which
they introduce themselves.

The violence of inscription.
Please stop sneaking to do that.
The downstairs neighbor already owns
the empathy you seek.

No longer compelled to cling
to that childish lingo, at last
I declare, as if speaking forthrightly
into a fearsome gale: "Cantilever."

That day human awareness permitted
untried sexual beatifications; adjectives
worthy of the scene were distributed
to those who could explain natural selection.

Your monsters are your business;
the intimate weird of your motor home.

The ghost brags about the speed
of its machine. Greasers drag combs
through the jet-black wind. A little dab will do
you when you need to be done to.

If grief is a cunning guest we should
hide the towels. Its insinuations
about the future erode my already scant
confidence in the utility of sublimation.

One glance & what had been known
was now *known*. From a chrysalis
of doubt, the fact they fucked
takes wing.

Photos of lakes & churches.
Albums full of such. Stale was
our daily bread.

I drew breath but it looked more
like wind. With so fast a pencil, the angle
of approach is everything.

Remember when we were actresses
who kissed men who were
ugly & wore cologne. Our whispers
wrapped around appetite.

Message on a sign above an empty
store & yes—tube socks were once
yours for a dollar ninety-nine.

Are you exempt from revision?
Maybe you walk
with the lord & his bullyboy gang.

Unsafe playground—that's where
the climax of my novel takes place.
Conflation of identities & violent reshaping
of colloquial speech then ensues.

Ah, literature. Me lifted by thee
wrongly.

Luxuriant secret—consumed then
disdained. Forever after
this yearning for incision.

No more pies; no more watering holes.
Hocus pocus is done for & it's smite time
for these dickhead prophets.

It's a question of proximity whether
or not the disguise works. Her tears
resplendent as mountain pools
even as much around her is masked
& much else remains unwashed.

This night, its perplexing hand grenade
of possibility. We brutes reek
of copulation & leave
behind a thread of nearly gold.

Snap fingers to turn any failure
to your best ever experience at the zoo—
to quote the setup instructions
I received with my new grail.

Would a solitary nail would do the trick?
Turns out I needed something
stronger: the glint of spite
in dirty eyes.

Slightest glance—yet the whole
contained in part, in a particle of that part.
Freeze frame on the recent disaster,
its lush bower. Grass bends in
air articulate.

Headlong in our pursuit of occult forms
we emulate those acolytes
who signed for the early-bird deal &
complimentary skin rejuvenator.

Arousal's your game? Go stomp the old sod,
expel that bad mojo. Only then may you
be suffused among expectant songs.

Begin with a length of rope—a thought
in readiness.
Society of dope fiends meets tonight at seven.
Helpless amid their orated absence.

Here comes the headache, the one
that weighs as much as last
week's compost & impresses upon
spectators the seriousness
with which we undertake its mission.

Save-a-penny jar or vending
machine: in which do you deposit
your faith in the woodsy folk?

I want to dig deeper. The curve
of the beast's horn
must *mean*.

At the memorial the candle's ferocity
is obscured from those in the cheap seats.

The more you claim fraudulence
as your excuse the more pumpkin-like
you appear when asked
to endure the paradise of immensity.

Her deletions—Joycean.

Money gripped me in its maw. I lived
to swindle dry cleaners.

Look, love reclines on the couch! Remember
the sins we lost in its cushions?

The lines on her forehead were a kind
of sacred script that mocked
lucidity. Had she filched her diction
from my insincerity?

These wrongdoers lost the many loves
that once sharpened the air between
their thighs & now find themselves unversed
in the tactile lore of nervous states.

Our last judgment—when the pain lets fall
through ev'ry lived hour. Present & past,
you realize, have been no more than a tease.

Being human: the film adaptation was better.

If the concealer works the damage is hardly
noticeable. Otherwise, the evidence is plain—
you have been misunderstood. Not quite sullen
but sunken, your face: an exhumation.

The pavement is a kind of elegy.
Or perhaps not.

The gods had hammers they say.
On my street there's a woman
who has a leaf blower.
An empyrean ruled by jerk-offs.

A bad crowd she fell in with. First the pill
popping & then she took up their critical
methodologies; so no surprise when I found her
later, alone & cursing the bathroom sink.

Regard this prince among empty men.
His robe of god's eyes, his mastery of all things
confessional. Upon the ocean of want
his navy plies its undulant course.

Dominion over the tides? Apply within.

The ideologue played snakes & ladders
with real snakes. When the upheaval he long
schemed for arrived his joy was boundless—
his mortifications could finally be proclaimed.

Soothed by correction from on high.
By the sweat of so beaten a brow comes
outward peace & the ability to simulate adequacy.

Exhaust me with your cunning ways.
I am recognized only by you & thus by you
wish to be meticulously tweezed.

Terrible words. All night of them.

Left to wander, I followed the sublime
until I nearly drowned in the heat
of so many undesired bodies
listless across my path.

The period is too meek to end my sentence.
A swipe of a scythe nicely
does the trick.

Can I plausibly grieve for the replica?

Long ago that mighty, mighty sword.
The father knelt; the son regarded
the throne. The laggard brother dismayed:
no guest could help him find a job.

Our soul gets its chances, you hear that said.
A solemn drumroll, then we scatter,
each with our own reprieve.

Mornings arrive with birdsong, sunset
brings insects. When the moment
is ripe we will standardize our spellings.

Monotonous this crisis. Philosophy
swells with its contentions.
But summon, if you will, a blemished
love once sighed behind the Dairy Queen.

I cried out for excess so went down
to the blessing mart to imbibe
the full import of vanished worlds.

Thus my story builds to murmur.

You're given teeth to chew
ache-heavy dreams; the doubts they leave
you swallow whole.

Last chance to pluck that phoenix
unworthy of its plumage.

Cupids huffing glue. Another season
of this & nothing newly born
will call this place home.

Unlike luxury, degradation requires
taste. What wouldn't I give to spit
in the palace & blame the fancy martyr?

The old rigmarole. How to get free of it?
Our first fear fractioned out
over a lifetime, its sum ever gathering.

"Smorgasbord" once mispronounced—a reason
for gnawing dismay?

She likes the nightlife, her consecration there.

The bloom lingers perhaps too long;
its smell of boredom, its pillowy years.

The word was *fondle*.

Her divinations depend on the antenna's
tilt, its posture within a whirl of causes.

Supply of award winners exceeds demand;
feather plucked dependencies!

You slather stars with unlovely paint
& expect applause from an audience
that only praises intentions.

Family-size portions—purgatory will be
a sweaty adventure.

Work those levers, Johnny joke-boy.
An impertinent fool is he who espouses a myth
about the faithful—their ascension despite
these sunny days of slo-mo duels.

Good hunch what's going on with you isn't
the same as what's going on with me.
On a silver platter: my apology's explanation.

This rust, these rags. Entranced
with furthermore.

Afflicted, aggrieved, we arrived at the castle
we'd dreamed of. Our pistols loose
in their holsters, our history convolute.

The genius wore out his welcome. Hand-
rolled cigarettes licked extravagantly.
He spoke shifty, sidewise
like he was practicing for prison.

Shallow pools grace the vale.
A mirage that abates the dilemma:
uninterrupted self.

Gomorrah? Maybe tomorrow.

Barechested atop the cliff, he waved his shirt
to signal how high he climbed. Most monstrous
sight—this mortal's exultation.

A masked woman arrives in a crowded room.
How many bedtime stories are we willing
to begin with that scene? The modern
temperament goes pitter-patter.

Syllables cast among the wretched. We watch
with foreboding as they assemble
a merciful diction.

Even asleep we deplete ourselves pursuing
velvety yet elusive neutralities.

Be wary in the mirrored house;
perception multiplies there.
Turn around then turn around again,
your conjugations blur.

Rinse, then implicate.

She stumbled, once more in the grip of emotion.
Beguiled by her wreckage, we itemized
for reimbursement later.

Tool of corrupt devising: the asterisk.
Our obscenities thus annotated
for ease of comprehension.

Unkind entries fill the dictionary you consult.
Your slushy enunciation of their vowels
turns the names of our hidden parts
into accusations.

Can there be certainty if there are
certainties? Stay very still so the bruises
that accompany such cogitation can be avoided.

This beard: its history as told by.

The insolent recluse photographed when drunk;
an unearthly choir mourns.

Smoke rises from the tuneless
forest as you lose your way, footprints fading
in snowfall. Your armored fame no use
amid this churn of shadows.

Expelled from Heliopolis, your flask
of balm left in a rental car.
Each deprivation in its own way
marvelous, you persevere.

The village blasphemer, the rest stop sage:
glorious form & motion marks them,
makes them the illuminati of our tedious era.

Have we been cleaved piece by pliable piece?
Does the creator even touch our clay?

Another sad room abandoned.
Soon the whole house is left behind
& resentment replaces loss.
In the damp, discolored sheets: the pungent
whiff of fabulation.

Confounded I am by yammering beasts,
their lack of dolorous cadence.

Among wished-for perfections, their stillness
a luxurious tedium. Credit cards, the filthy
talk. Remedies abound for that skulking
snitch we call expression.

Slow dance in the fateful gym—tracks
of tears, tears on a pillow.

Roll up your sleeves & narrate, punk.

Apply moisture to activate these ashes.
Face aglow with spoiled might,
the tyrant mind doth screw itself.

Simulacrum of loss before the keening
thing itself. Nights of nothing more
where, in time, we will surely be found.

A wretched stranger fell prostrate at her door.
All perils, she assured him, will be swept away.
O shining bit of breath a promise is.

Me in action—a marionette whose flailing
limbs mock my ardent ascent.

Arrayed beneath a sky stretched taut
the seeming dead, their faces turned
from earth to falling light.

How song is thought is vertical is emptied out
yet brimming still. How much like
unused things we be.

The stove's blue-green flame swells
beneath the kettle; another stint
in the mild yoke, this soul more bent, etcetera.

You look and look but the mirror
remains unchanged. The mouth
is ruined by silence, the gaze will not
relinquish its obdurate pity.

My sleep-soaked theories scarcely breathe.
Felicity.

Acknowledgments

I am grateful to the editors and publishers of the magazines in which versions of these poems first appeared: the *Big Other*, *Brooklyn Rail*, *Hambone*, *Literary Hub*, *Seneca Review*, the *Scofield*, *Southampton Review*; "The Triumph of Poverty" appeared in *The Triumph of Poverty: Poems Inspired by the Work of Nicole Eisenman* (Off the Park Press); "Categories of Apprehension" and "Informal Lull" were each included in artist's books produced by Mark Schlesinger. And, once again, thank you, John Yau.

About the Author

Albert Mobilio is the recipient of a Whiting Award, a MacDowell Fellowship, and an Andy Warhol Foundation Arts Writers Grant. His work has appeared in *Bookforum*, *Black Clock*, *BOMB*, *Cabinet*, *Hambone*, *Harper's*, *Open City*, *Paris Review Daily*, and *Tin House*. Books of poetry include *Bendable Siege*, *The Geographics*, *Me with Animal Towering*, and *Touch Wood*. A book of fiction, *Games and Stunts*, was published in 2017. He is an associate professor of literary studies at The New School and serves as a coeditor of *Hyperallergic Weekend*.